D1115009

Motherhood

∎

With 17 full-color
illustrations

RUNNING PRESS
PHILADELPHIA · LONDON

Library of Congress Cataloging-in-Publication Number
90–53465

ISBN 0–89471–983–1

This book may be ordered by mail from the publisher.
Please include $1.00 for postage and handling.
But try your bookstore first!
Running Press Book Publishers, 125 South Twenty-second
Street, Philadelphia, Pennsylvania 19103–4399

Introduction

■ ■ ■

They wipe our noses when we're three, dry our tears when we're fourteen, and calm our fears when we're twenty. Seemingly inexhaustible as a source of comfort and support, mothers have the ability to understand us when no one else will.

The inseparable bond between mother and child begins at the moment of conception, growing and developing as mother and child grow and learn together.

All women, whether or not they are mothers, represent the potential of human life. In these quotations women share their thoughts and experiences. Humorous, tender and loving, the selections in this book provide poignant insights into the challenges and rewards of motherhood.

. . . IT IS STILL THE

biggest gamble in the world.

It is the glorious life force. It's

huge and scary—it's an act of

infinite optimism.

GILDA RADNER (1946–1989)
American comedian

I BEGIN TO LOVE THIS

little creature, and to

anticipate his birth as a fresh

twist to a knot, which I do

not wish to untie.

■

MARY WOLLSTONECRAFT
(1759–1797)
English writer

NO ONE HAD TOLD HER
what it would be like, the way
she loved her children. What
a thing of the body it was, as
physically rooted as sexual
desire, but without its edge of
danger.

MARY GORDON, b. 1949
American writer

I REMEMBER LEAVING
the hospital . . . thinking,
"Wait, are they going to let
me just walk off with him? I
don't know beans about
babies! I don't have a license
to do this. [We're] just
amateurs."

ANNE TYLER, b. 1941
American writer

LIFE IS THE FIRST GIFT,

love is the second, and

understanding the third.

MARGE PIERCY, b. 1934
American writer and poet

I STOOD IN THE
hospital corridor the night
after she was born. Through
a window I could see all the
small, crying newborn infants
and somewhere among them
slept the one who was mine.
I stood there for hours filled
with happiness until the night
nurse sent me to bed.

LIV ULLMAN, b. 1939
Norwegian actress and writer

WHILE YOU CAN

quarrel with a grownup, how
can you quarrel with a
newborn baby who has
stretched out his little arms
for you to pick him up?

MARIA VON TRAPP (1905–1987)
Austrian-born entertainer
and writer

LOVE TWISTED

suddenly. . .inside her,
compelling her to reach into
the crib and lift up the moist,
breathing weight. . . . The
smells of baby powder and
clean skin and warm flannel
mingled with the sharp scent
of wet nappy.

ROSIE THOMAS
20th-century English writer

PARENTS OF YOUNG

children should realize that

few people, and maybe no

one, will find their children as

enchanting as they do.

BARBARA WALTERS, b. 1931
American journalist

I ACTUALLY REMEMBER
feeling delight, at two o'clock
in the morning, when the
baby woke for his feed,
because I so longed to have
another look at him.

MARGARET DRABBLE, b. 1939
English writer

. . .WHO IS GETTING

more pleasure from this

rocking, the baby or me?

NANCY THAYER, b. 1943
American writer

IN THE SHELTERED
simplicity of the first days
after a baby is born, one sees
again the magical closed
circle, the miraculous sense of
two people existing only for
each other.

ANNE MORROW LINDBERGH,
b. 1906
American writer

. . . A BABE AT THE

breast is as much pleasure as

the bearing is pain.

MARION ZIMMER BRADLEY,
b. 1930
American writer

WHEN A CHILD ENTERS

the world through you, it

alters everything on a

psychic, psychological and

purely practical level.

JANE FONDA, b. 1937
American actress

WHEN YOU HAVE A

baby, you set off an explosion in your marriage, and when the dust settles, your marriage is different from what it was. Not better, necessarily; not worse, necessarily; but different.

NORA EPHRON, b. 1941
American writer

IF A CHILD IS TO KEEP
alive his inborn sense of
wonder he needs the
companionship of at least
one adult who can share it,
rediscovering with him the
joy, excitement and mystery
of the world we live in.

RACHEL CARSON (1907–1964)
American biologist

I LOOKED ON CHILD

rearing not only as a work of
love and duty but as a
profession that was fully as
interesting and challenging as
any honorable profession in
the world and one that
demanded the best that I
could bring to it.

ROSE KENNEDY, b. 1890
American mother

. . . THE WALKS AND
talks we have with our two-
year-olds in red boots have a
great deal to do with
the values they will cherish
as adults.

EDITH F. HUNTER, b. 1919
American writer

THE DARN TROUBLE

with cleaning the house is it

gets dirty the next day

anyway, so skip a week if you

have to. The children are the

most important thing.

BARBARA BUSH, b. 1925
First Lady of the United States

TEDDY BEARS

shouldn't sit in closets when

there's a child around who

will love them.

JANET DAILEY, b. 1944
American writer

DOES IT SEEM

impossible that the child will grow up? That the bashful smile will become a bold expression . . . that a briefcase will replace the blue security blanket?

ANNE BEATTIE, b. 1947
American writer

SEEING YOU SLEEPING
peacefully on your back
among your stuffed ducks,
bears and basset hounds
would remind me that no
matter how good the next
day might be, certain
moments were gone
forever. . . .

JOAN BAEZ, b. 1941
American singer

I LOVE BEING A MOTHER

. . . I am more aware. I feel
things on a deeper level. I
have a kind of understanding
about my body, about being
a woman.

SHELLEY LONG, b. 1949
American actress

A WOMAN WHO CAN

cope with the terrible twos

can cope with anything.

JUDITH CLABES
20th-century American editor

TRUTH, WHICH IS

important to a scholar, has

got to be concrete. And there

is nothing more concrete

than dealing with babies,

burps and bottles, frogs and

mud.

■

JEAN J. KIRKPATRICK, b. 1926
American diplomat

I GOT MORE CHILDREN

than I can rightly take care of,

but I ain't got more

than I can love.

OSSIE GUFFY, b. 1931
American writer

LITTLE CHILDREN

are still the symbol of

the eternal marriage between

love and duty.

◼

GEORGE ELIOT (1819–1880)
English writer

I SAW PURE LOVE WHEN

my son looked at me, and I

knew that I had to make a

good life for the two of us. . .

SUZANNE SOMERS, b. 1950
American actress

LOVING A CHILD

doesn't mean giving in to all his whims; to love him is to bring out the best in him, to teach him to love what is difficult.

NADIA BOULANGER
(1887–1979)
French musician and teacher

THERE IS NO INFLUENCE

so powerful as that of the

mother.

SARAH JOSEPHA HALE
(1788–1879)
American pioneer and writer

WHEN YOU ARE A
mother, you are never really
alone in your thoughts. You
are connected to your child
and to all those who touch
your lives. A mother always
has to think twice, once
for herself and once
for her child.

SOPHIA LOREN, b. 1934
Italian actress

ALL THE EARTH,

though it were full of kind

hearts, is but a desolation

and a desert place to a

mother when her only child

is absent.

ELIZABETH GASKELL
(1810–1865)
English writer

BEING A MOTHER,

as far as I can tell, is a

constantly evolving process of

adapting to the needs of your

child while also changing and

growing as a person in your

own right.

DEBORAH INSEL, b. 1949
American writer

. . . THERE'S A LOT MORE

to being a woman than being

a mother, but there's a hell of

a lot more to being a mother

than most people suspect.

■

ROSEANNE BARR, b. 1952
American comedian and actress

TO LOVE THE TENDER

heart hath ever fled,

As on its mother's breast the

infant throws

Its sobbing face, and there in

sleep forgets its woe.

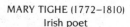

MARY TIGHE (1772–1810)
Irish poet

. . .WHAT DO GIRLS DO

who haven't any mothers to

help them through their

troubles?

LOUISA MAY ALCOTT
(1832–1888)
American writer and editor

MUMMY HERSELF HAS
told us that she looked upon
us more as her friends than
her daughters. Now that is all
very fine, but still, a friend
can't take a mother's place. I
need my mother as an example
which I can follow, I want to
be able to respect her.

ANNE FRANK (1929–1945)
German diarist

THE MOTHER IS THE

medium through which the

primitive infant transforms

himself into a socialized

human being.

BEATA RANK (1896–1967)
American psychologist

TO TALK TO A CHILD, TO
fascinate him, is much more
difficult than to win an
electoral victory. But it is
more rewarding.

COLETTE (1873–1954)
French writer

ANY MOTHER COULD

perform the jobs of several

air traffic controllers

with ease.

LISA ALTHER, b. 1944
American writer

DO NOT, ON A RAINY
day, ask your child what he
feels like doing, because I
assure you that what he feels
like doing, you won't feel like
watching.

FRAN LEBOWITZ, b. 1950
American writer

THE REAL MENACE IN

dealing with a five-year-old

is that in no time at all

you begin to sound like a

five-year-old.

JEAN KERR, b. 1923
American playwright

IT GOES WITHOUT

saying that you should never

have more children than you

have car windows.

ERMA BOMBECK, b. 1927
American writer

THE BEST WAY TO KEEP

children at home is to make

home a pleasant atmosphere

—and to let the air out

of the tires.

DOROTHY PARKER (1893–1967)
American writer

YOU HAVE A

wonderful child. Then, when he's 13, gremlins carry him away and leave in his place a stranger who gives you not a moment's peace.

JILL EIKENBERRY
20th-century American actress

THERE IS NOTHING

more thrilling in this world, I

think, than having a child that

is yours, and yet is

mysteriously a stranger.

AGATHA CHRISTIE (1890–1976)
English writer

. . . EVERY MOTHER OF
more than one child has a
secret favorite, so secret that
she might go through her
whole life and never admit
to herself which one it was.
Sometimes it takes a crisis,
something out of the
ordinary, to make her realize
her preference.

GAIL GODWIN, b. 1937
American writer

I FOLD THE DRAB

maternity pants with the

frayed elastic waistband and

place them back in the box.

Then I put the box away—

for now.

CAROL KORT. b. 1945
American writer

THE THIRD BABY IS THE
easiest. . . . You know, for
instance, how you're going to
look in a maternity dress
about the seventh month,
and you know how to release
the footbrake on a baby
carriage without fumbling
amateurishly. . .

SHIRLEY JACKSON (1919–1965)
American writer

I LEARNED SO MUCH

more about men by having

a son.

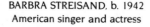

BARBRA STREISAND, b. 1942
American singer and actress

IF YOU WANT A BABY,

have a new one. Don't baby

the old one.

JESSAMYN WEST (1907–1984)
American writer

WERE WOMEN MEANT

to do everything—work *and*

have babies?

CANDICE BERGEN, b. 1946
American actress

I THINK WE'RE SEEING IN
working mothers a change
from "Thank God It's Friday"
to "Thank God It's Monday."
If any working mother has
not experienced that feeling,
her children are not
adolescent.

ANN DIEHL
20th-century American university
administrator

A SUCCESSFUL CAREER

means nothing without a

personal life. So, the children

were always with me.

JANET LEIGH, b. 1927
American actress

ONE OF MY CHILDREN

wrote in a third-grade piece

on how her mother spent her

time...''one-half time on

home, one-half time on

outside things, one-half time

writing.''

■

CHARLOTTE MONTGOMERY
20th-century American writer

MY EVOLUTION INTO

a politician developed

not in opposition to my role

as a mother, but as an

extension of it.

MADELEINE KUNIN, b. 1933
American politician

THE MOTHER IS THE

most precious possession of
the nation, so precious that
society advances its highest
well-being when it protects
the functions of the mother.

ELLEN KEY (1849–1926)
Swedish writer

IF MOTHERHOOD IS AN occupation which is critically important to society the way we say it is, then there should be a mother's bill of rights.

BARBARA ANN MIKULSKI,
b. 1936
American politician

WHEN PEOPLE ASK ME
what I do, I always say I am a
mother first. Your children
represent your thoughts. Your
children are a statement.

JACQUELINE JACKSON, b. 1944
American activist

YOUR CHILDREN ARE

always your "babies," even if

they have gray hair.

JANET LEIGH, b. 1927
American actress

OUR CHILDREN ARE NOT going to be just "our children"—they are going to be other people's husbands and wives and the parents of our grandchildren.

MARY S. CALDERONE, b. 1904
American physician and writer

CHILDREN ARE LIKELY

to live up to what you believe

of them.

LADY BIRD JOHNSON, b. 1912
Former First Lady of the
United States

WHEN I STOPPED SEEING

my mother with the eyes of a

child, I saw the woman who

helped me give birth to

myself.

NANCY FRIDAY, b. 1937
American writer

MY FIRST JOB IS TO BE A

good mother.

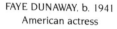

FAYE DUNAWAY, b. 1941
American actress

THERE IS SO MUCH TO

teach, and the time goes

so fast.

■

ERMA BOMBECK, b. 1927
American writer

IF YOU MUST GIVE YOUR child lessons, send him to driving school. He is far more likely to end up owning a Datsun than he is a Stradivarius.

◾

FRAN LEBOWITZ, b. 1950
American writer

MOST MOTHERS ARE

instinctive philosophers.

HARRIET BEECHER STOWE
(1811–1896)
American writer

PART OF THE GOOD PART

of being a parent is a

constant sense of *déjà vu*. But

some of what you have to *vu*

you never want to *vu* again.

ANNA QUINDLEN
20th-century American writer

THE QUICKEST WAY FOR

a parent to get a child's

attention is to sit down and

look comfortable.

■

LANE OLINHOUSE
20th-century American writer

THE PHRASE "WORKING

mother" is redundant.

■

JANE SELLMAN
20th-century American writer

CLEANING YOUR HOUSE

while your kids are still

growing is like shoveling the

walk before it stops snowing.

PHYLLIS DILLER, b. 1917
American comedian

WHEN YOU WORK WITH
adults, you're working with
people who are usually
rational and make an effort to
keep some sort of schedule.
When you have a child, just
the opposite happens: things
are unscheduled, chaotic.

WENDY SCHUMAN
20th-century American editor

. . .THE ESSENTIAL
thing about mothers—one
needs to know that they are
there, particularly at that age
when, paradoxically, one is
trying so hard to break away
from parental influence.

MARGOT FONTEYN, b. 1919
English dancer

MY MOTHER WANTED

me to be her wings, to fly as

she never quite had the

courage to do. I love her for

that. I love that she wanted to

give birth to her own wings.

ERICA JONG, b. 1942
American poet and writer

WOMEN AS THE
guardians of children possess
great power. They are the
molders of their children's
personalities and the arbiters
of their development.

■

ANN OAKLEY, b. 1944
English sociologist

A MOTHER IS NOT A person to lean on but a person to make leaning unnecessary.

■

DOROTHY CANFIELD FISHER
(1879–1958)
American writer

A MOTHER IS NEITHER

cocky, nor proud, because
she knows the school
principal may call at any
minute to report that her
child had just driven a
motorcycle through the
gymnasium.

MARY KAY BLAKELY, b. 1957
American writer

THERE IS A POINT

where you aren't as much

mom and daughter as you

are adults and friends.

JAMIE LEE CURTIS, b. 1959
American actress

WE ARE TOGETHER, MY
child and I. Mother and child,
yes, but *sisters* really, against
whatever denies us all that
we are.

ALICE WALKER, b. 1944
American writer

I WOULD LIKE THEM

to be the happy end of

my story.

MARGARET ATWOOD. b. 1939
Canadian writer

MY ONLY ADVICE IS TO

stay aware, listen carefully

and yell for help if you

need it.

JUDY BLUME, b. 1938
American writer

IT WILL BE GONE

before you know it. The

fingerprints on the wall

appear higher and higher.

Then suddenly they

disappear.

DOROTHY EVSLIN, b. 1923
American writer

FOR ME, MOTHERHOOD
has been the one true, great,
and wholly successful
romance. It is the only love I
have known that is expansive
and that could have stretched
to contain with equal passion
more than one object . . . .

IRMA KURTZ, b. 1935
American writer

I WAS NOT A CLASSIC
mother. But my kids were
never palmed off to boarding
school. So, I didn't bake
cookies. You can buy cookies,
but you can't buy love.

RAQUEL WELCH, b. 1940
American actress

THE PRESIDENCY IS

temporary—but the family is

permanent.

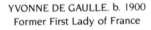

YVONNE DE GAULLE, b. 1900
Former First Lady of France

LOVING A CHILD IS A

circular business . . . the more

you give, the more you get,

the more you get, the more

you want to give.

PENELOPE LEACH, b. 1937
American writer

This book has been bound using handcraft methods,
and Smyth-sewn to ensure durability.

The text was edited by Jill M. Ward.
The dust jacket was designed by Toby Schmidt.
The interior was designed by Judith Barbour Osborne.
The illustrations were researched by Gillian Speeth.
The type was set in Novarese by Commcor
Communications Corporation.

Front cover:

Mary Cassatt, *Mother and Child*. Private collection.
Giraudon/Art Resource, New York.

Back cover:

Auguste Renoir, *Gabrielle and Jean*. Paris, Orangerie.
Art Resource, New York.

Interior illustrations:

Berthe Morisot, *The Cradle*, 1872. Paris, Musée d'Orsay.
Scala/Art Resource, New York.

Edouard Vuillard, *Public Gardens* (detail). Paris, Musée
d'Orsay. Giraudon/Art Resource, New York.